Healthy Plates

DAIRY

VALERIE BODDEN

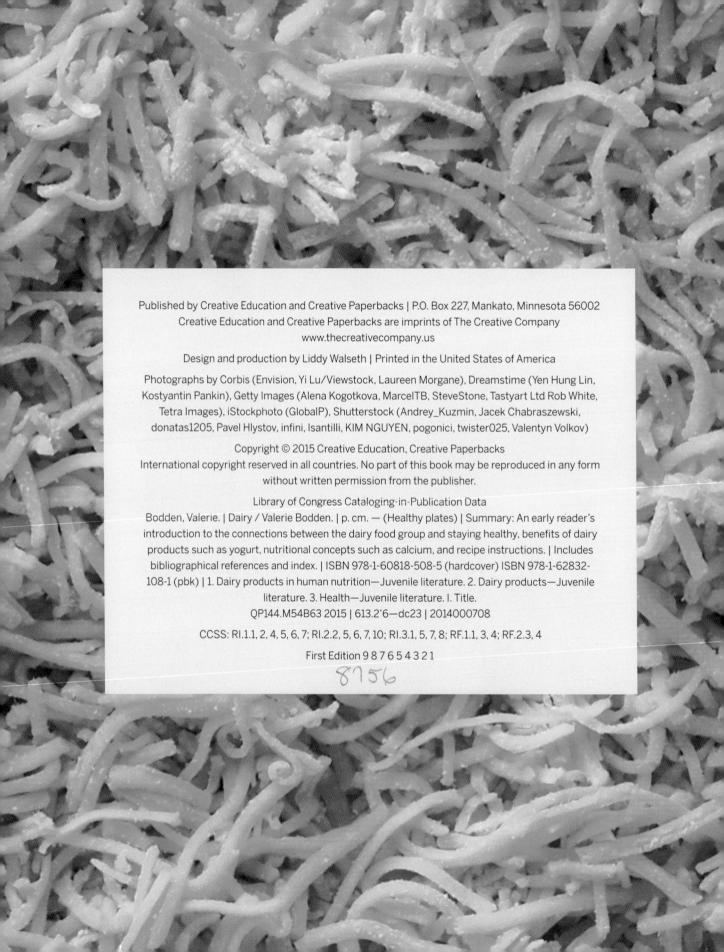

Published by Creative Education and Creative Paperbacks | P.O. Box 227, Mankato, Minnesota 56002
Creative Education and Creative Paperbacks are imprints of The Creative Company
www.thecreativecompany.us

Design and production by Liddy Walseth | Printed in the United States of America

Photographs by Corbis (Envision, Yi Lu/Viewstock, Laureen Morgane), Dreamstime (Yen Hung Lin, Kostyantin Pankin), Getty Images (Alena Kogotkova, MarcelTB, SteveStone, Tastyart Ltd Rob White, Tetra Images), iStockphoto (GlobalP), Shutterstock (Andrey_Kuzmin, Jacek Chabraszewski, donatas1205, Pavel Hlystov, infini, Isantilli, KIM NGUYEN, pogonici, twister025, Valentyn Volkov)

Library of Congress Cataloging-in-Publication Data
Bodden, Valerie. | Dairy / Valerie Bodden. | p. cm. — (Healthy plates) | Summary: An early reader's introduction to the connections between the dairy food group and staying healthy, benefits of dairy products such as yogurt, nutritional concepts such as calcium, and recipe instructions. | Includes bibliographical references and index. | ISBN 978-1-60818-508-5 (hardcover) ISBN 978-1-62832-108-1 (pbk) | 1. Dairy products in human nutrition—Juvenile literature. 2. Dairy products—Juvenile literature. 3. Health—Juvenile literature. I. Title.
QP144.M54B63 2015 | 613.2'6—dc23 | 2014000708

CCSS: RI.1.1, 2, 4, 5, 6, 7; RI.2.2, 5, 6, 7, 10; RI.3.1, 5, 7, 8; RF.1.1, 3, 4; RF.2.3, 4

First Edition 9 8 7 6 5 4 3 2 1

8756

TABLE OF CONTENTS

THERE ARE MANY DIFFERENT KINDS OF HEALTHY FOODS TO TRY!

Growing Up

Your body needs food to give it energy and help it grow. But not all foods are good for you. Healthy foods contain the **nutrients** (*NOO-tree-unts*) your body needs to be at its best. Healthy foods are put into five food groups: dairy, fruits, **grains**, **proteins**, and vegetables. Your body needs foods from each food group every day.

Dairy Group

Milk and foods made from milk are in the dairy group. Cheese is part of the dairy group. So are yogurt and ice cream.

MANY DAIRY PRODUCTS ARE MADE FROM COWS' MILK.

Vitamins and Nutrients

Dairy foods give your body **vitamins** and a nutrient called calcium. Calcium helps build strong bones and teeth. Milk has Vitamin D, too. Vitamin D helps your body use calcium.

A 1-OUNCE (28.3 G) SLICE OF CHEDDAR CHEESE HAS 204 MIL-LIGRAMS OF CALCIUM.

Dairy foods have Vitamin A to help you see well. B vitamins in dairy foods help your body turn food into energy. They keep your brain and heart healthy, too.

NUTS AND SEEDS FROM THE PROTEIN GROUP ARE HEART-HEALTHY FOODS.

Dairy foods also have protein to help your body grow. They have potassium, too. This nutrient helps make your heart healthy by keeping your **blood pressure** low.

13

Some dairy foods also contain **fat**. Too much fat is not good for your body. Kids aged two and older should drink fat-free (skim) milk or low-fat milk. But younger kids need the fat in whole milk to help their brains grow.

LOWER-FAT MILK AND WHOLE MILK HAVE THE SAME AMOUNT OF CALCIUM.

How Much?

Most kids should get two to three cups (473–710 ml) of dairy foods a day. Two ounces (56.7 g) of cheese counts as one cup of dairy.

People who are older or more active can eat more dairy foods. People who cannot eat dairy can have **soy** milk, yogurt, or cheese.

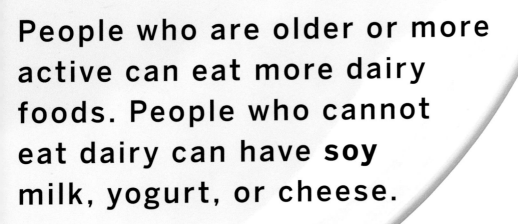

Healthy Living

You can make sure you get enough dairy products by drinking milk with your meals. Or you can have yogurt for a snack. Try some frozen yogurt for dessert.

ADDING MILK AND YOGURT TO CEREAL PACKS A LOT OF DAIRY INTO BREAKFAST.

Eating dairy foods is part of being healthy. Exercising is another part. Try to move your body an hour every day. Exercising and eating healthy can be fun—and can make you feel good, too!

JUMPING AROUND AND RIDING A BIKE ARE FUN WAYS TO EXERCISE.

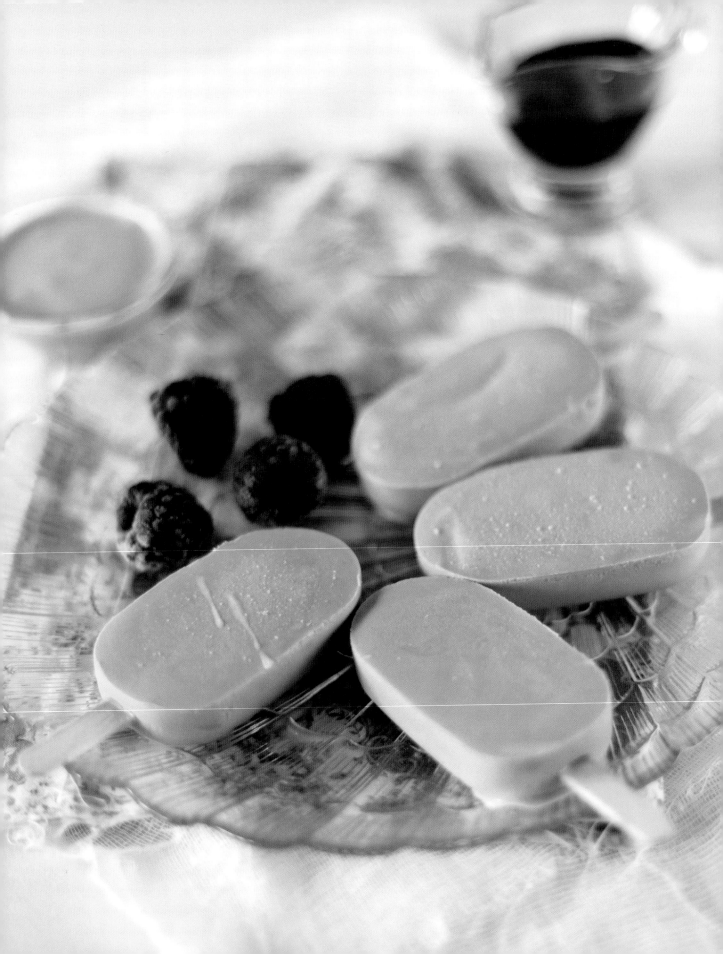

MAKE A DAIRY SNACK:

FROZEN YOGURT POPS

1 CUP VANILLA YOGURT
½ CUP STRAWBERRIES
(CHOPPED), BLUEBERRIES,
OR RASPBERRIES

Mix the yogurt and berries in a bowl. Pour the mixture into small plastic cups. Cover with foil. Poke a spoon into the middle of each cup. The handle should stick out the top of the foil. Put the cups in the freezer. Soon you will have a healthy dairy snack!

GLOSSARY

blood pressure—how hard a person's blood pushes against the blood vessels, or tubes that carry blood through the body

fat—a nutrient that provides and stores energy in the body

grains—parts of some kinds of grasses, such as wheat or oats, that are used to make bread and other foods

nutrients—the parts of food that your body uses to make energy, grow, and stay healthy

proteins—foods such as meat and nuts that contain the nutrient protein, which helps the body grow

soy—made from the seeds of the soybean plant

vitamins—nutrients found in foods that are needed to keep your body healthy and working well

READ MORE

Head, Honor. *Healthy Eating.* Mankato, Minn.: Sea-to-Sea, 2013.

Kalz, Jill. *Dairy Products.* North Mankato, Minn.: Smart Apple Media, 2004.

Llewellyn, Claire. *Healthy Eating.* Laguna Hills, Calif.: QEB, 2006.

WEBSITES

My Plate Kids' Place
http://www.choosemyplate.gov/kids/index.html
Check out games, activities, and recipes about eating healthy.

PBS Kids: Healthy Eating Games
http://pbskids.org/games/healthyeating.html
Play games that help you learn about healthy foods.

Note: Every effort has been made to ensure that the websites listed above are suitable for children, that they have educational value, and that they contain no inappropriate material. However, because of the nature of the Internet, it is impossible to guarantee that these sites will remain active indefinitely or that their contents will not be altered.

INDEX